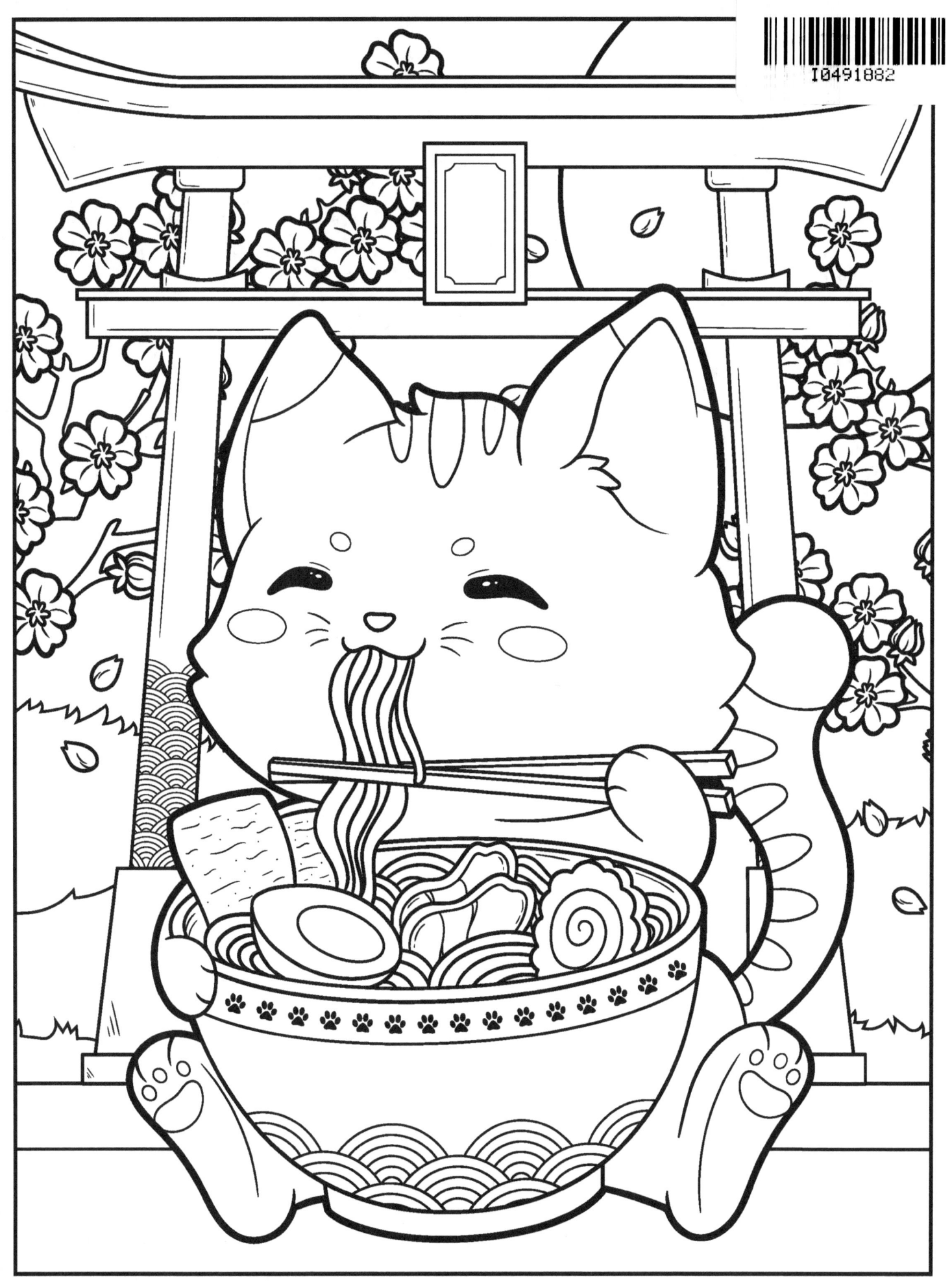

I0491882

Ramen Animals Coloring Book © 2021 by CC Coloring
Art by : Leriza May Marinās

All rights reserved. No part of this book may be used or reproduced in any manner
whatsoever without written permission except in the case of brief quotations
embodied in critical articles and interviews.

First edition: 2021

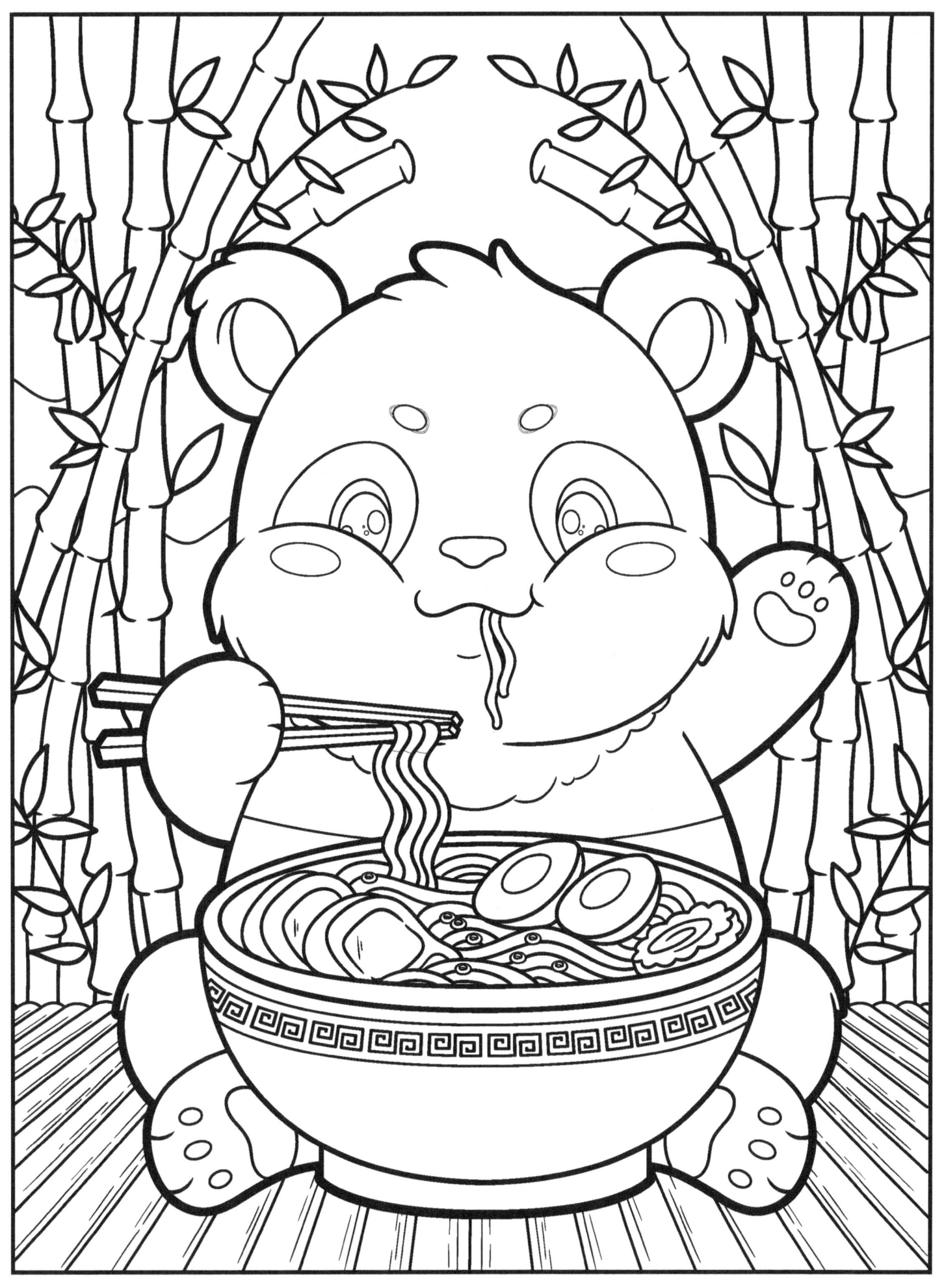

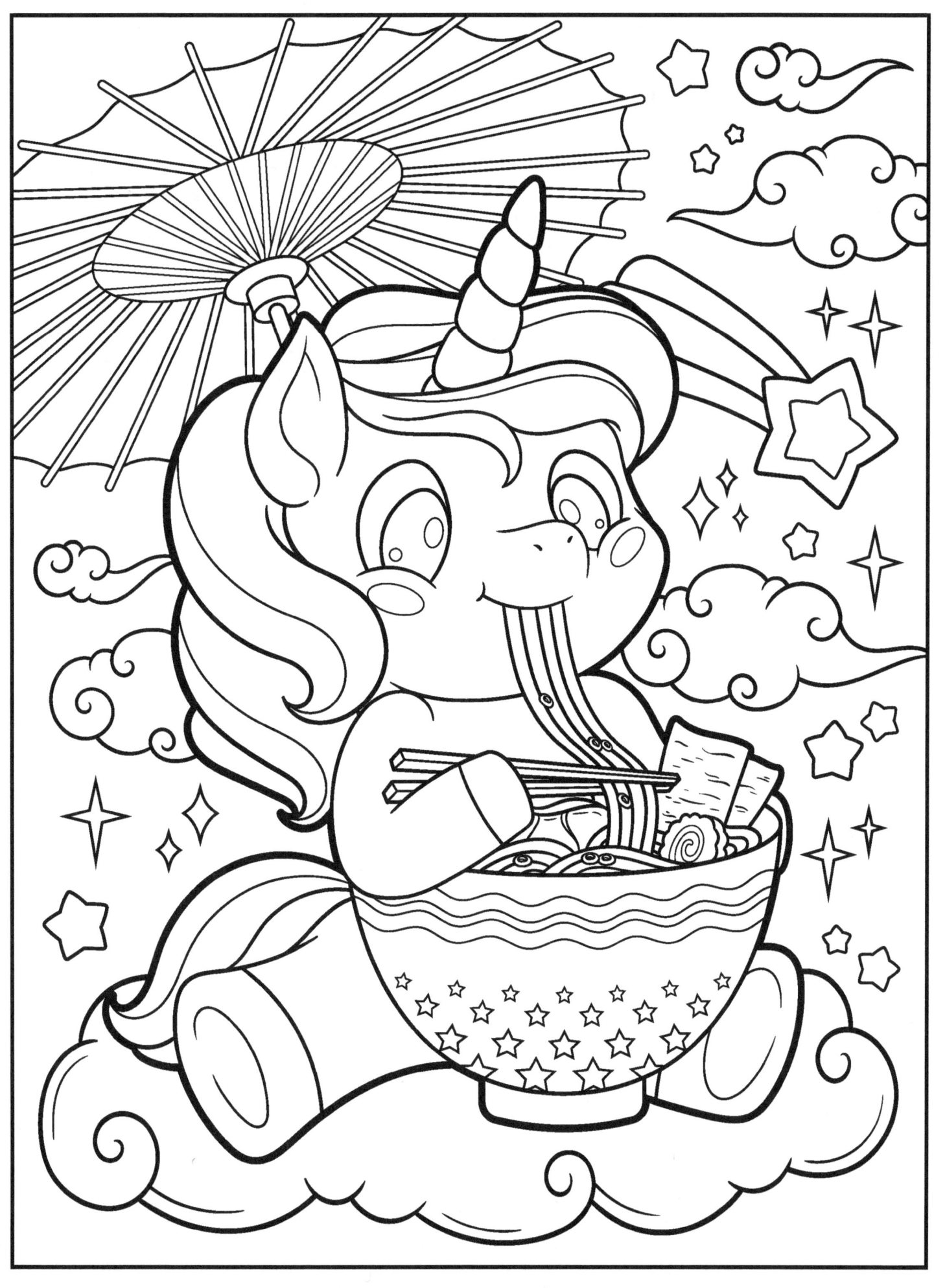

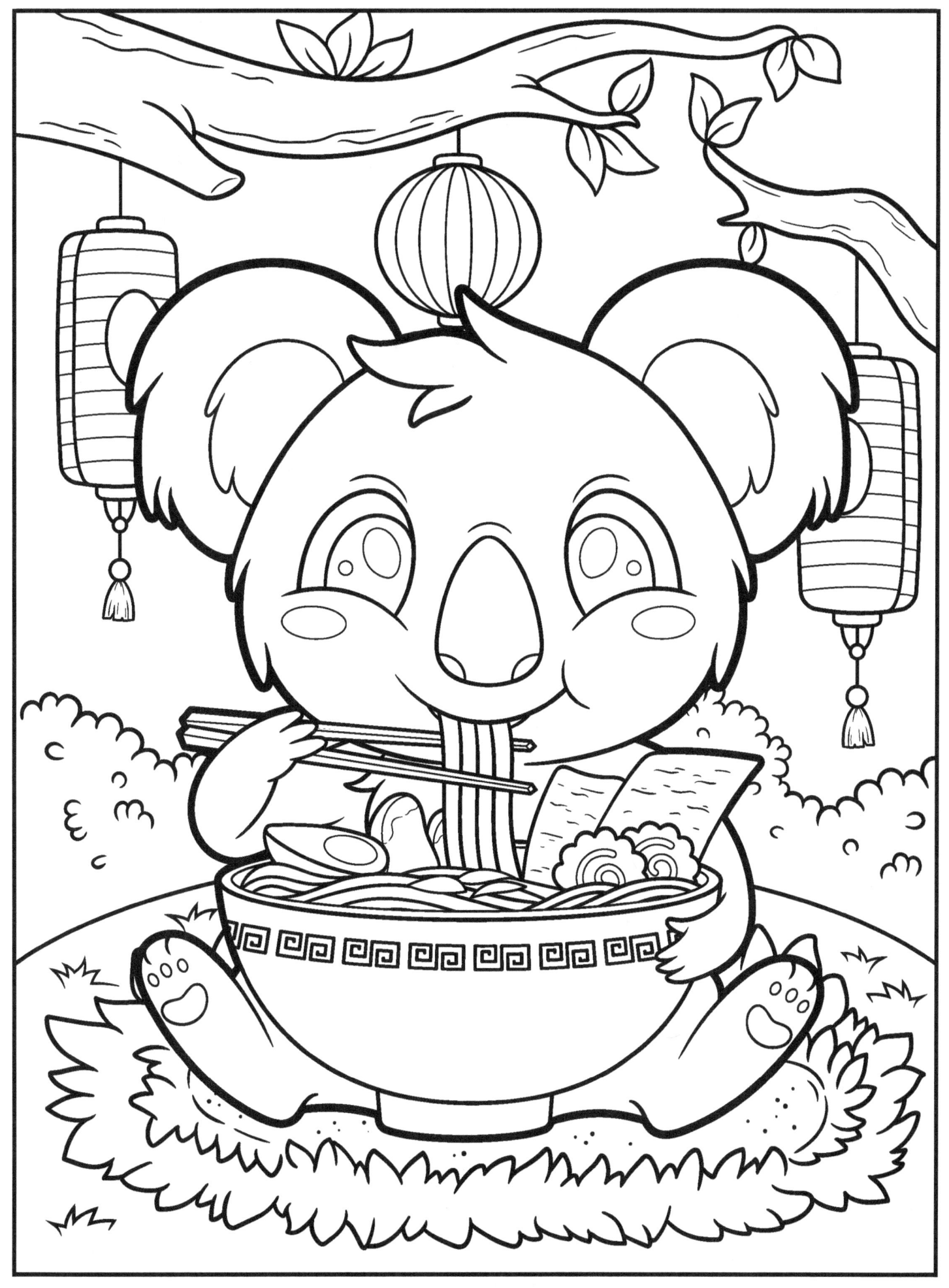

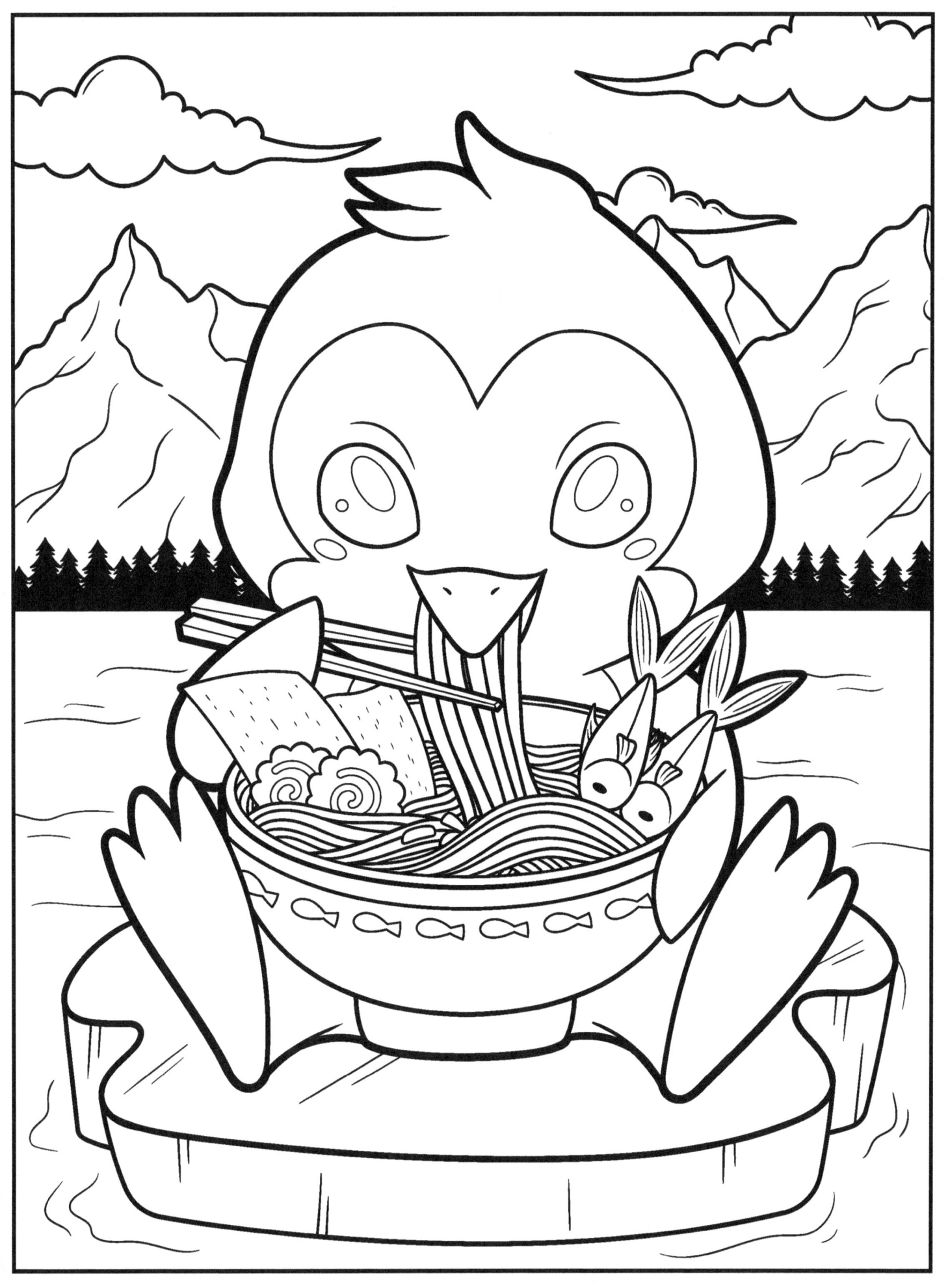

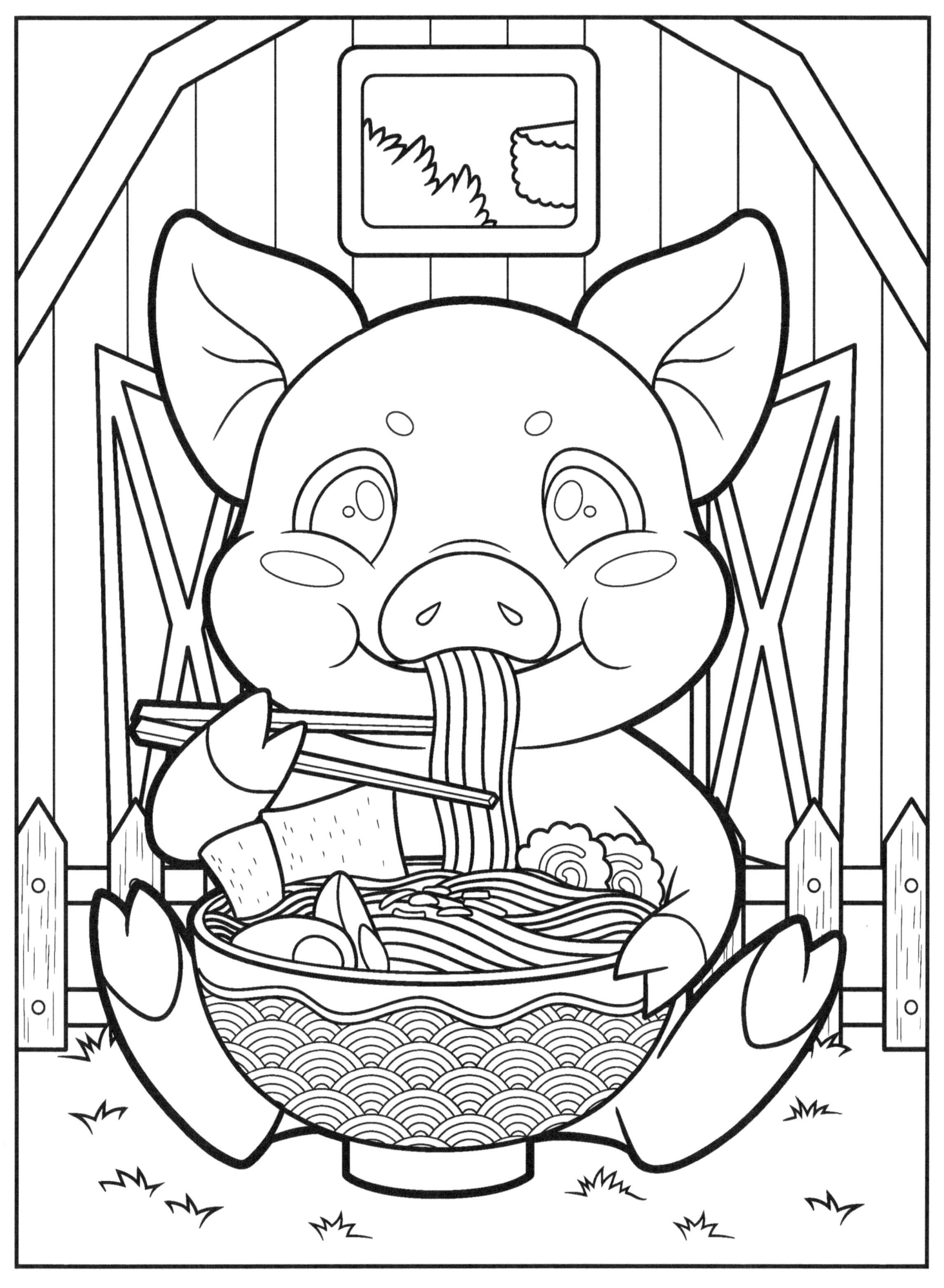

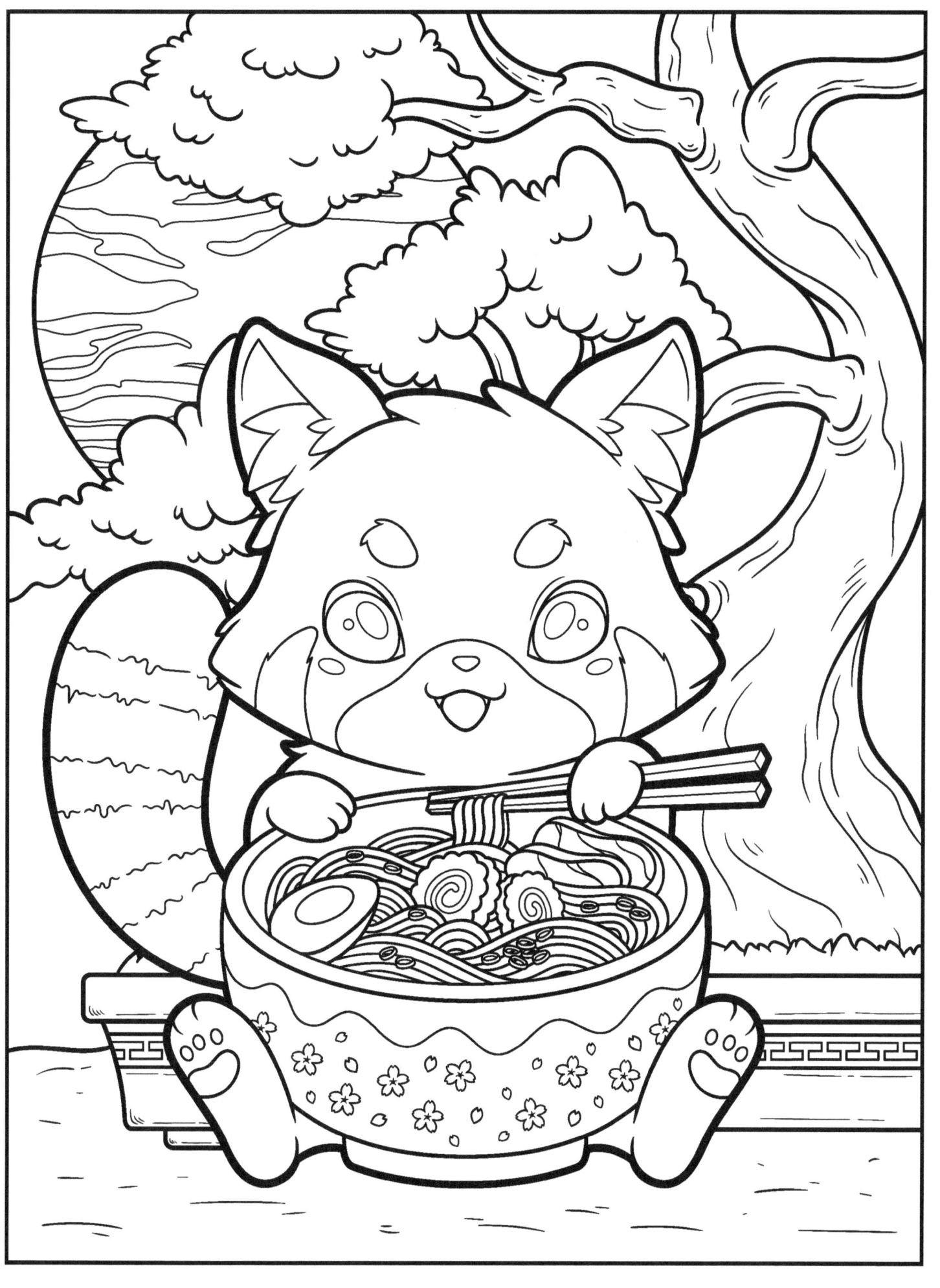

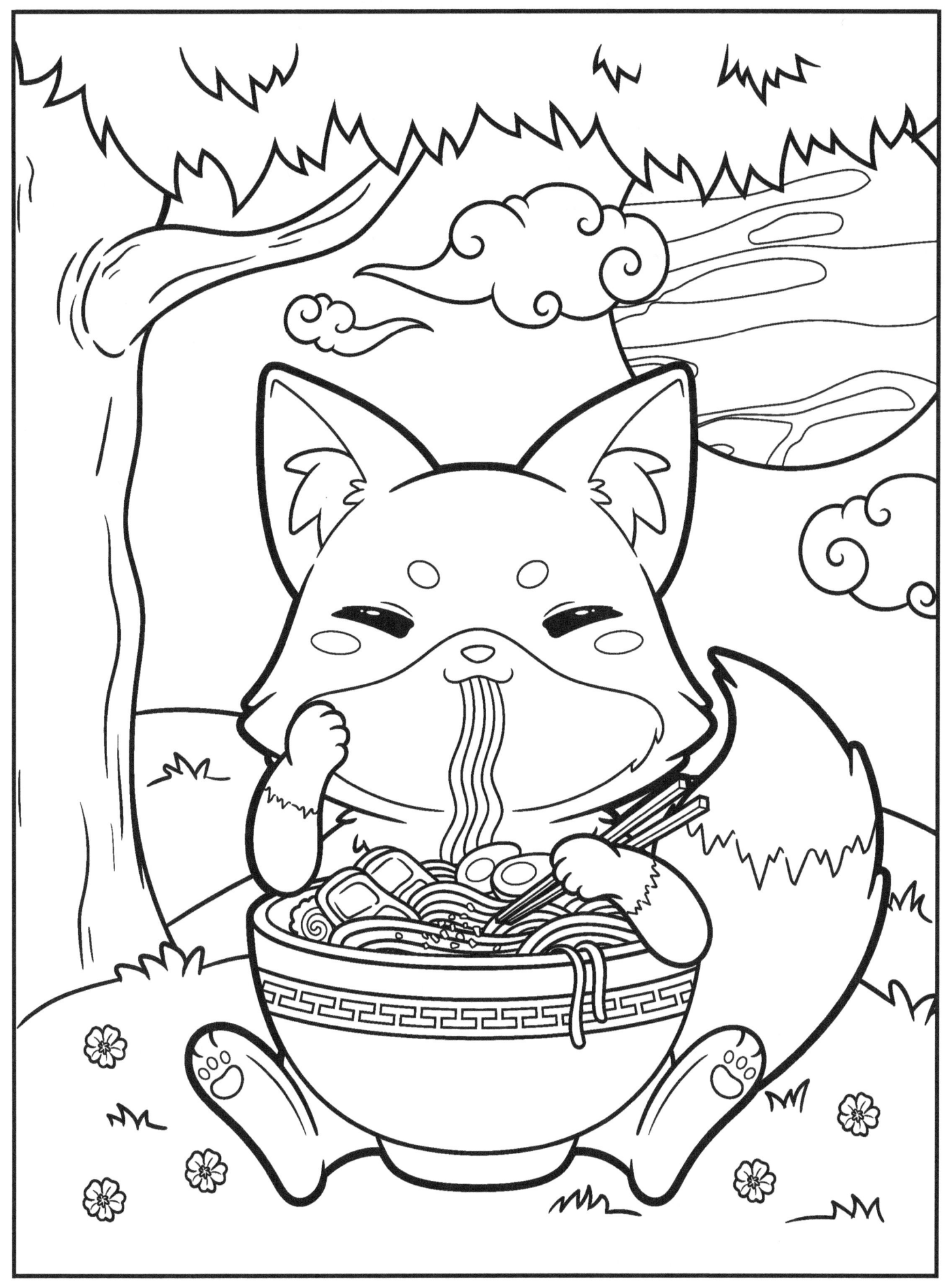

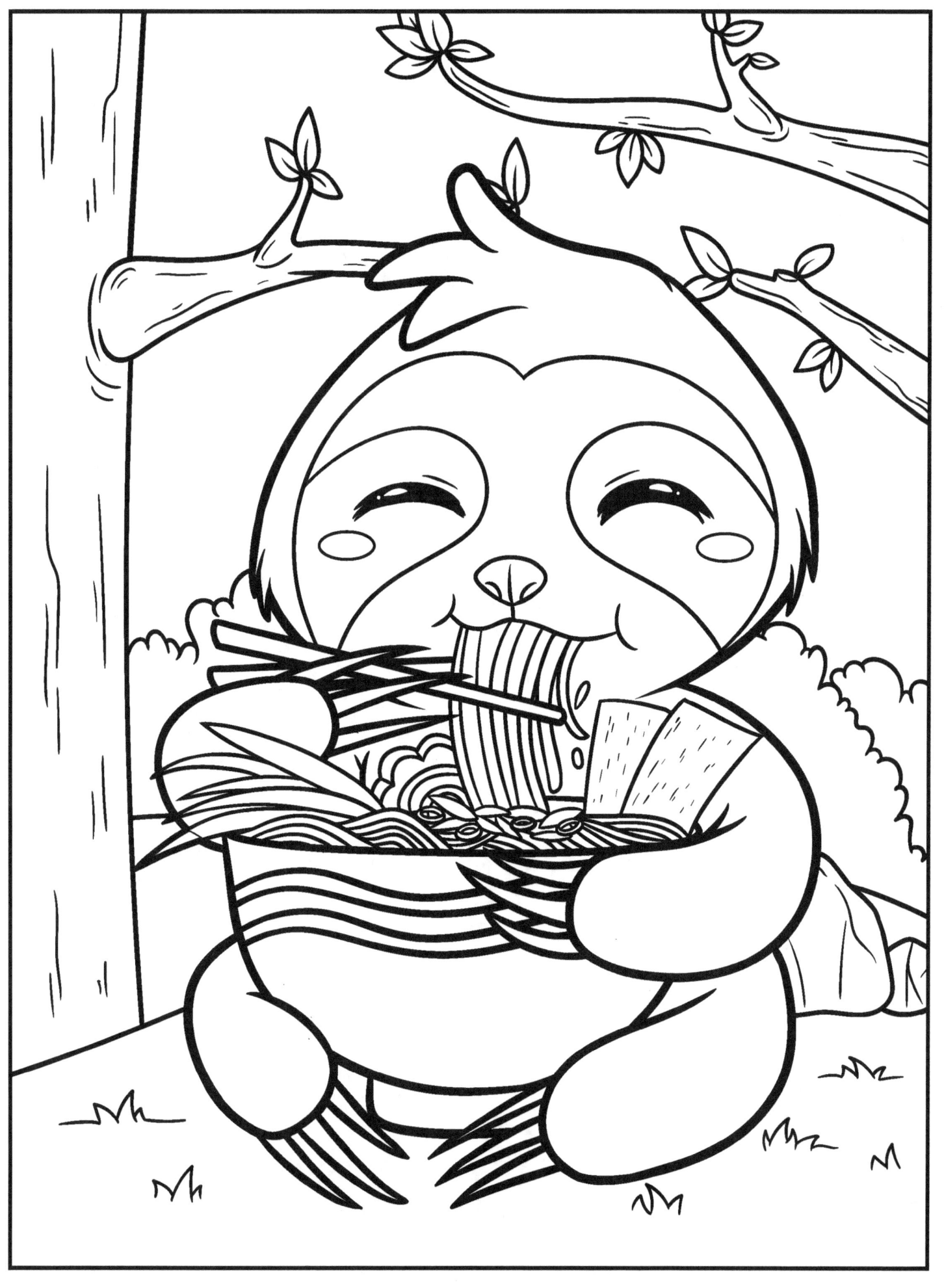

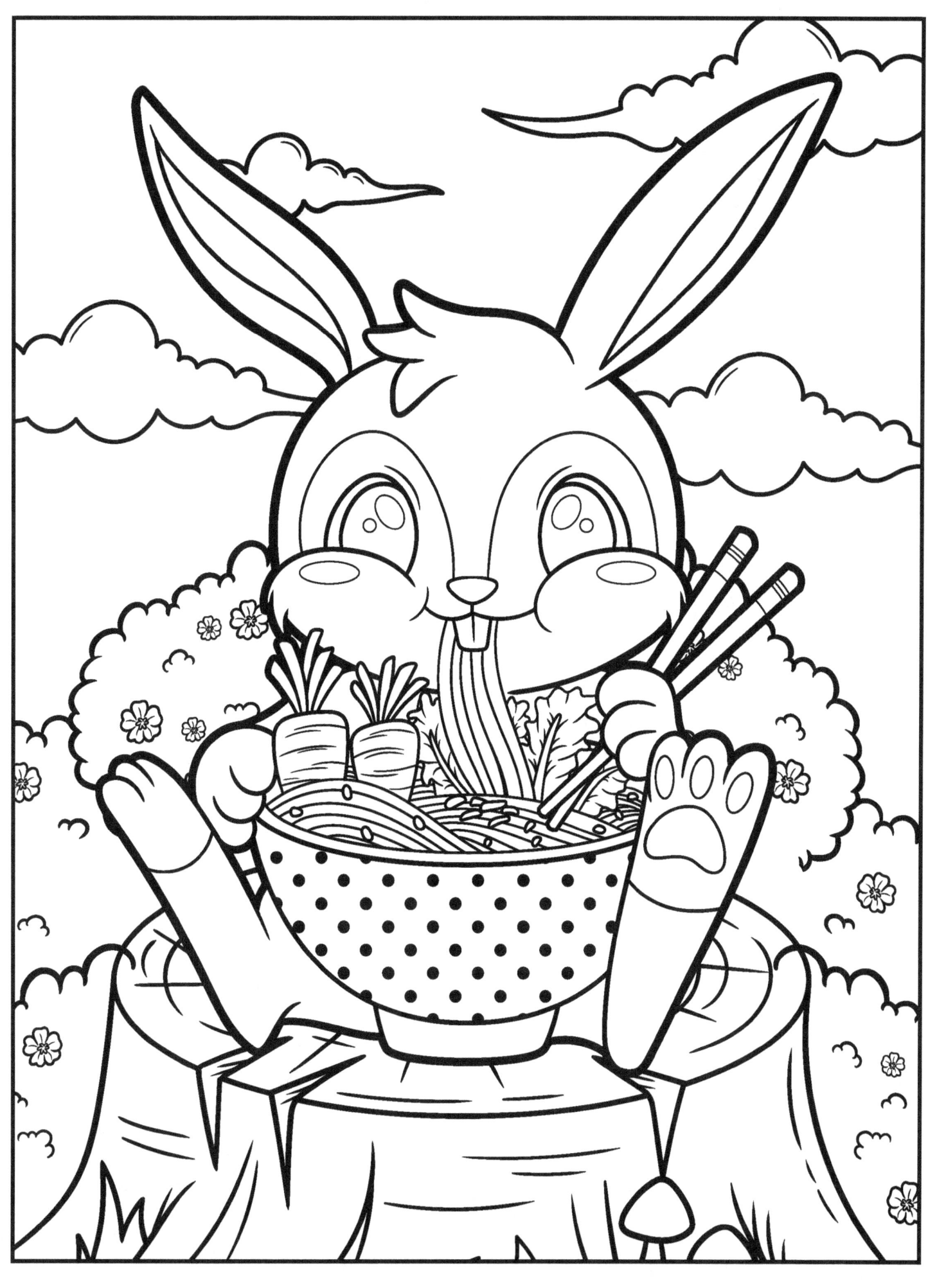

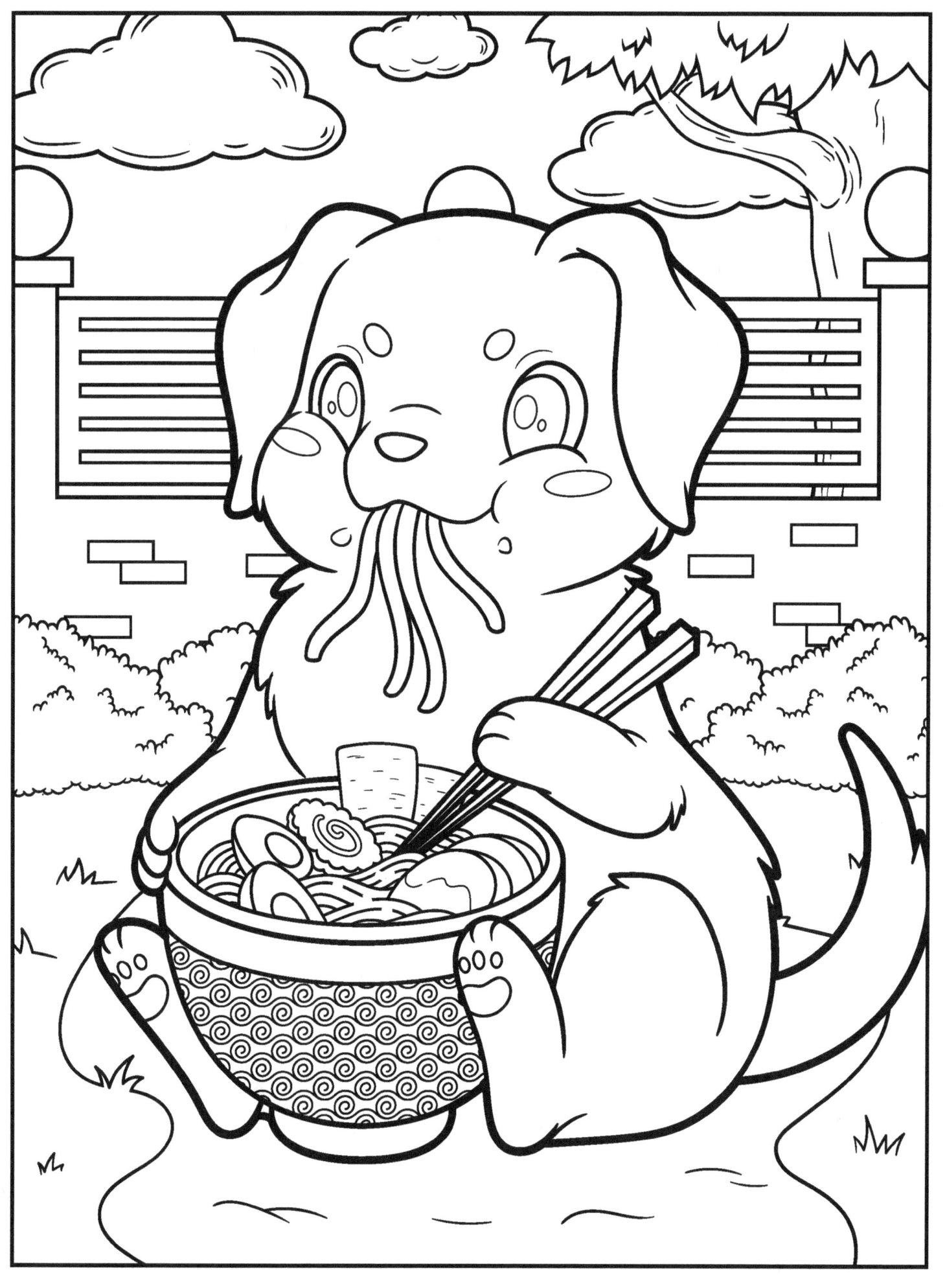

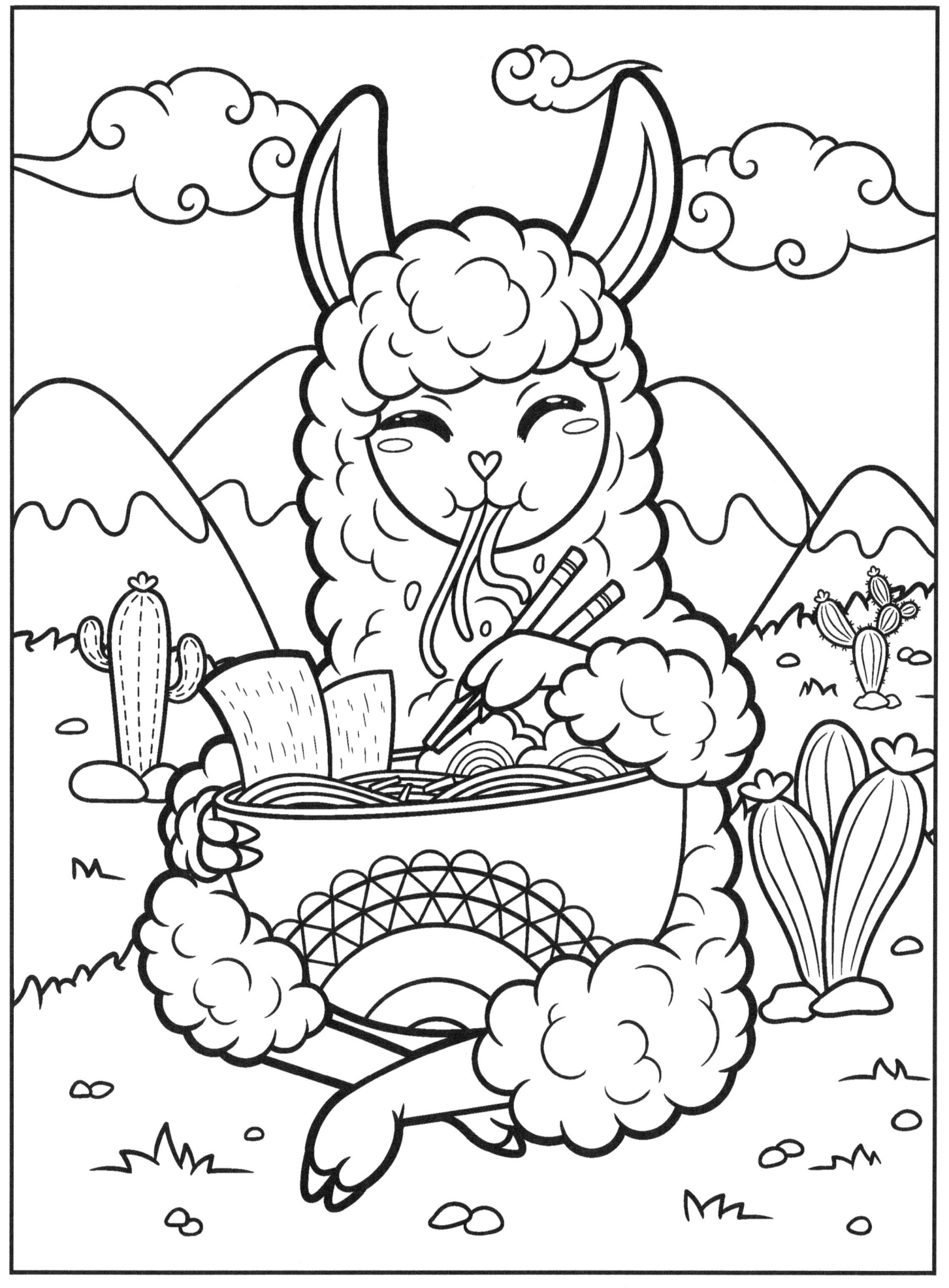

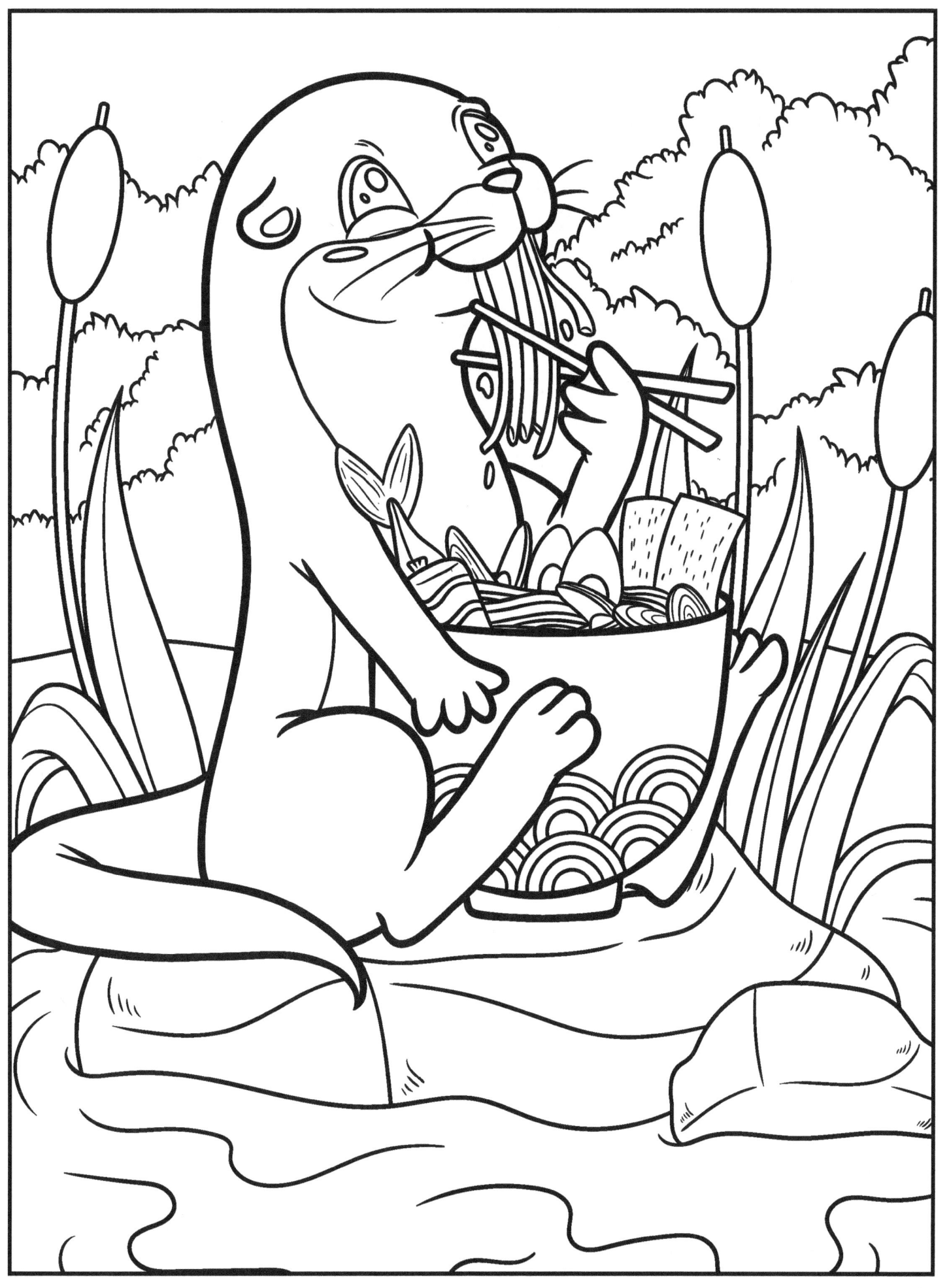

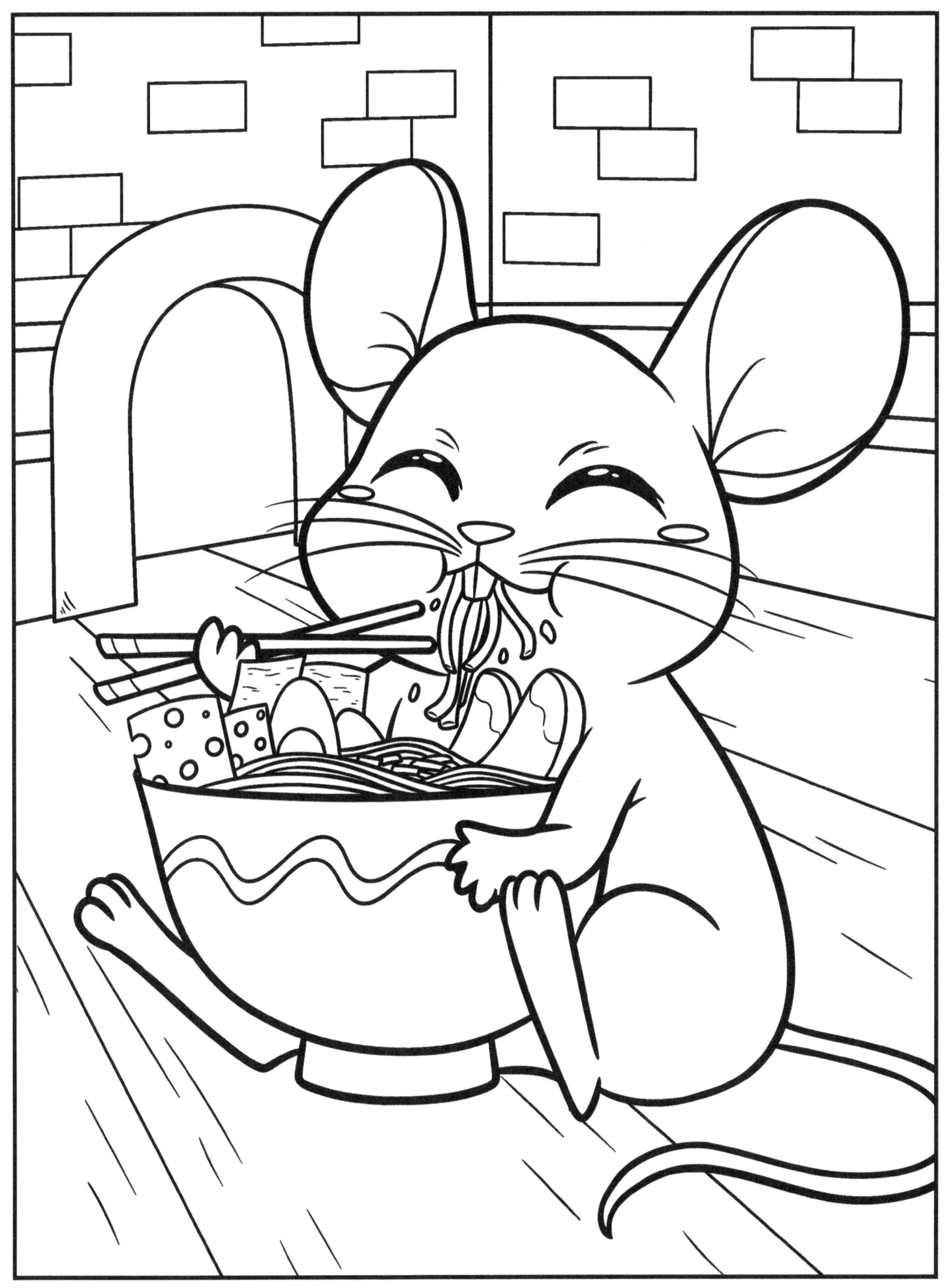

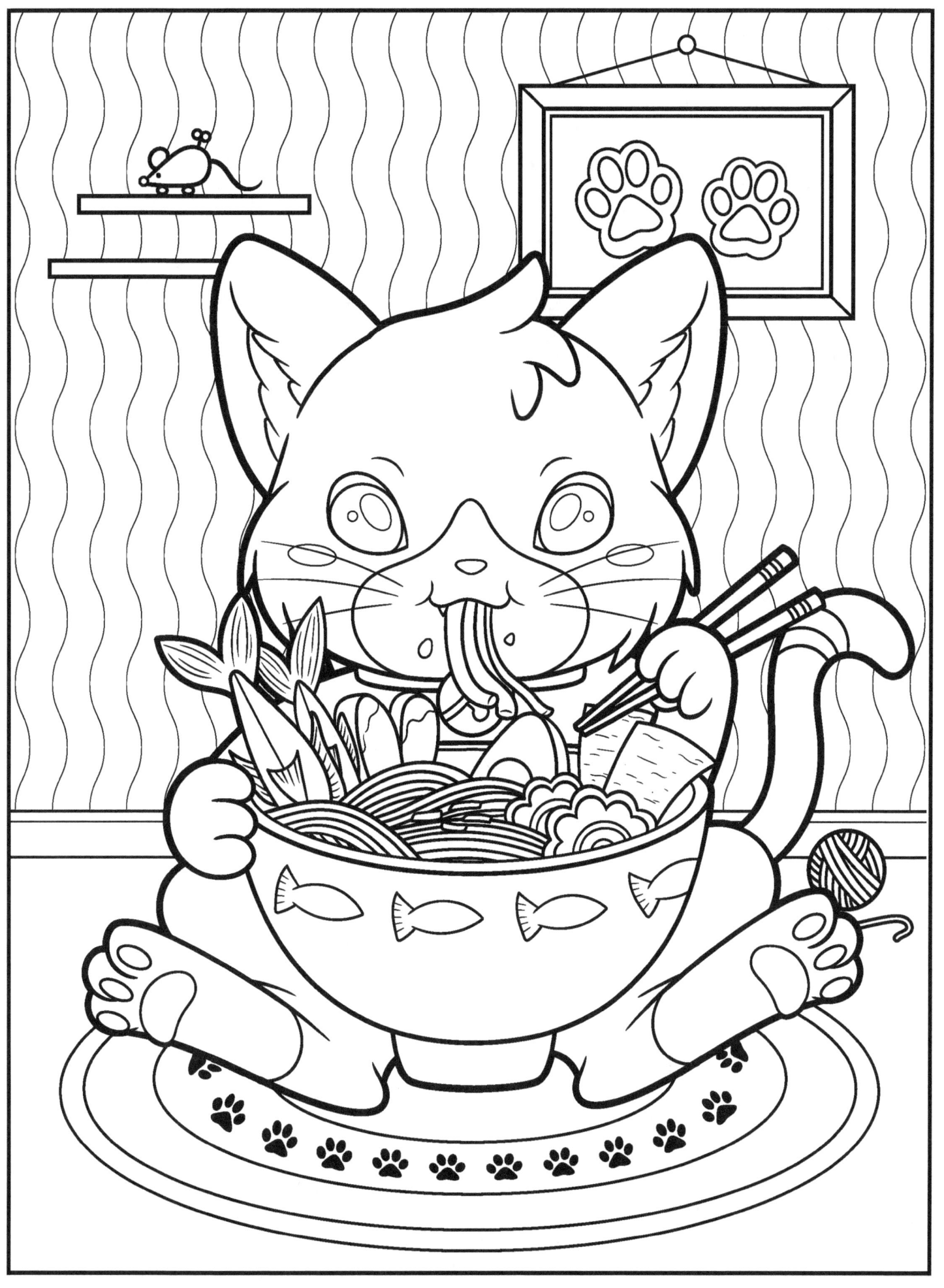

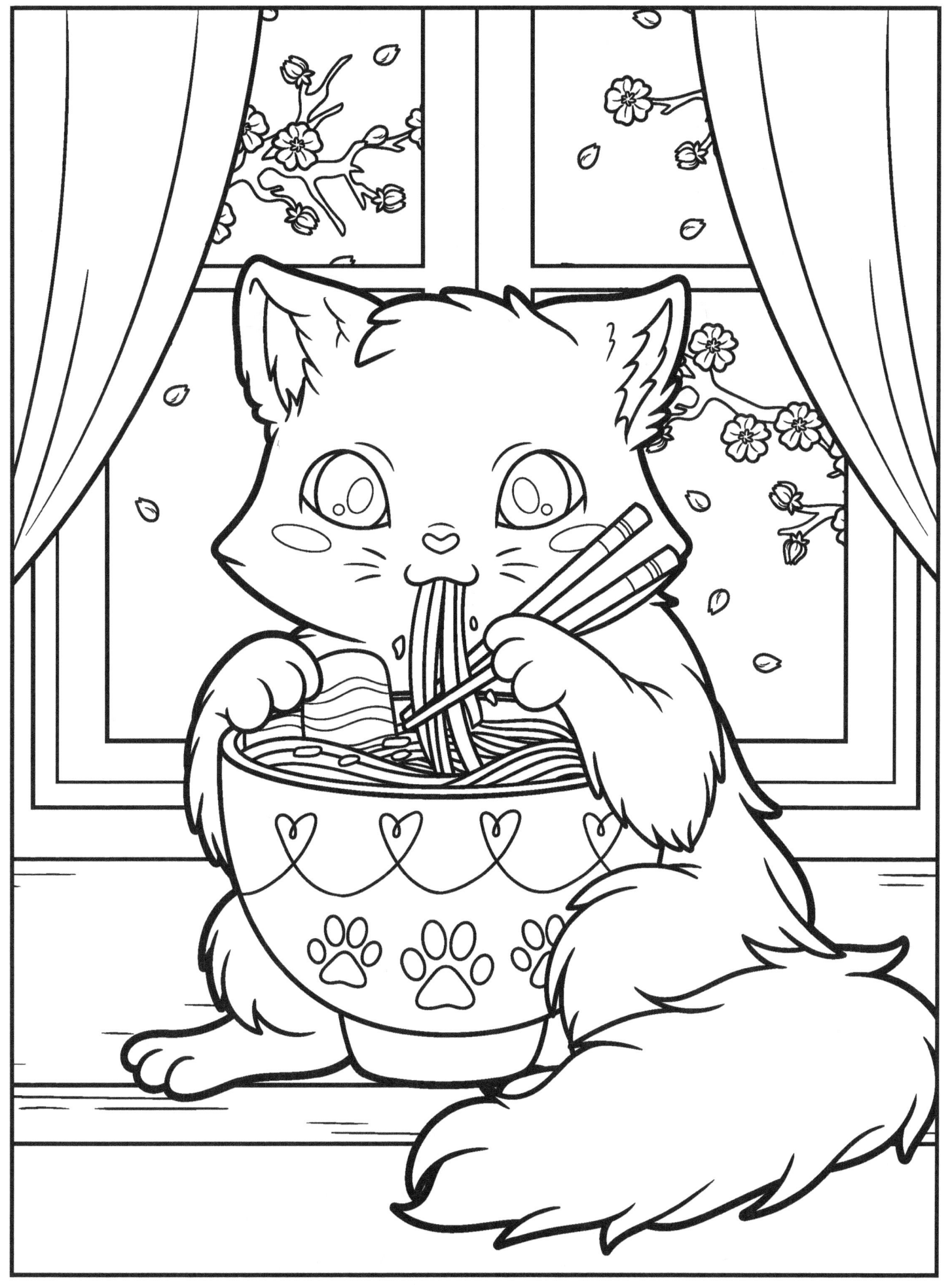

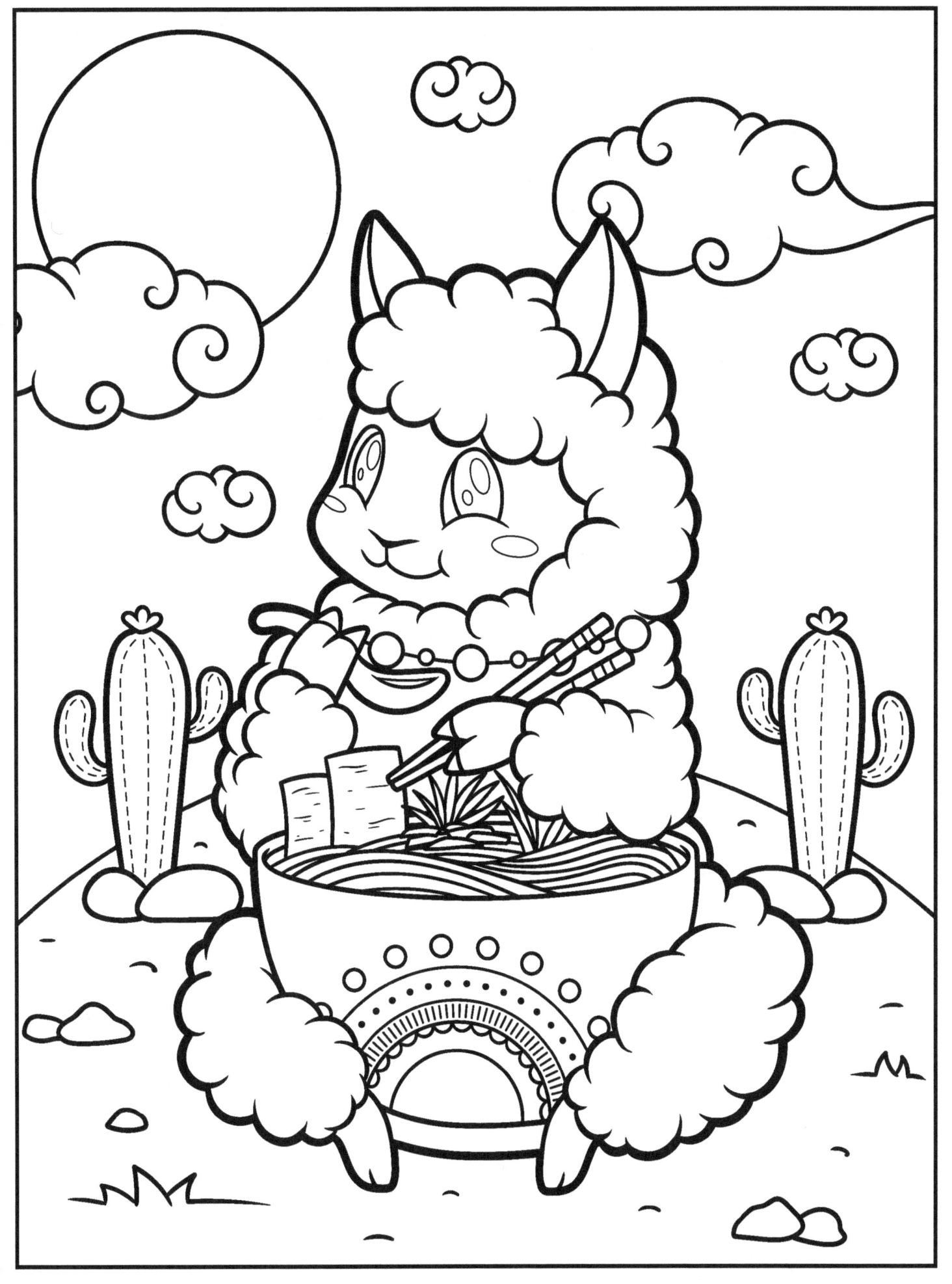

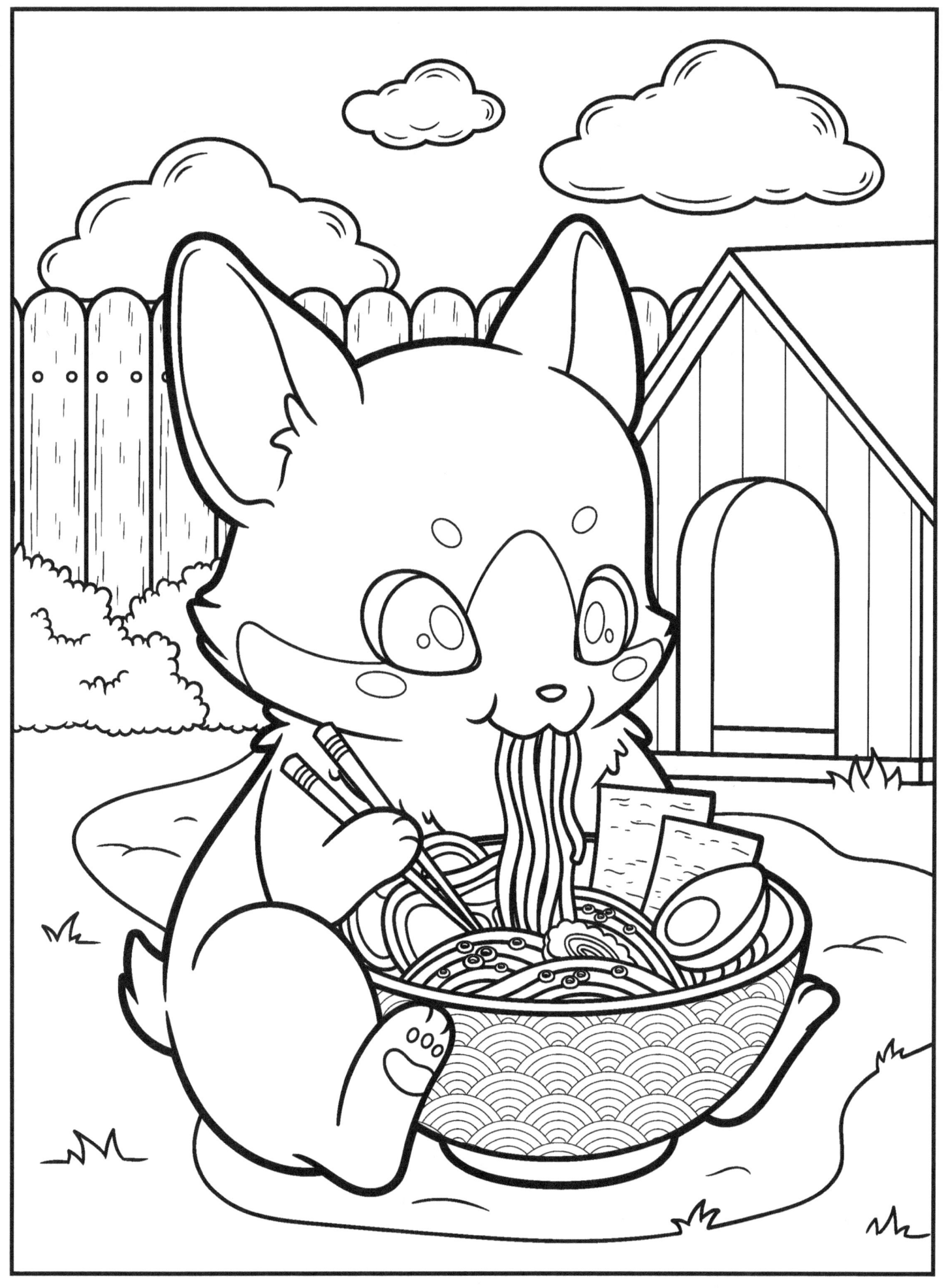

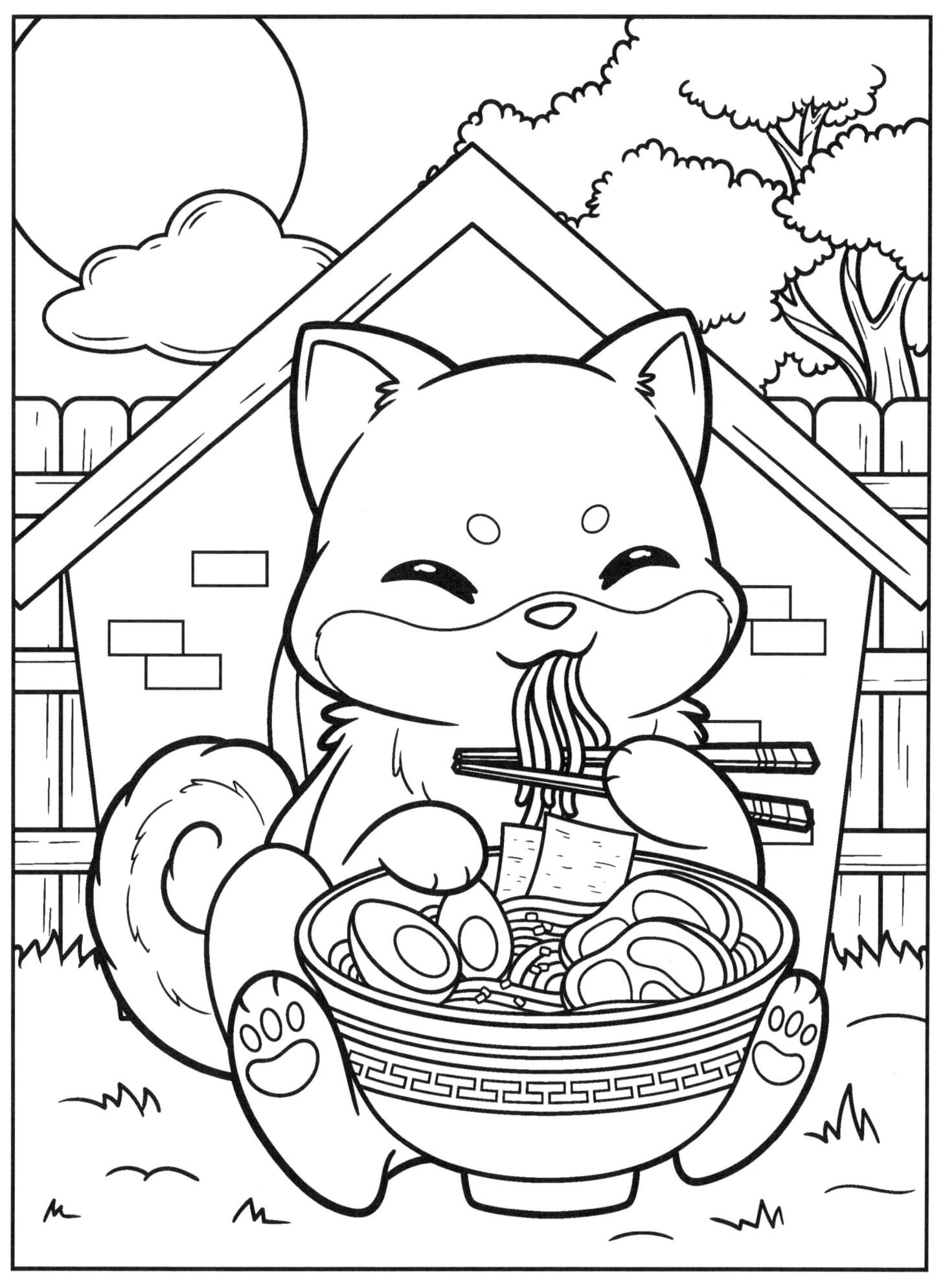

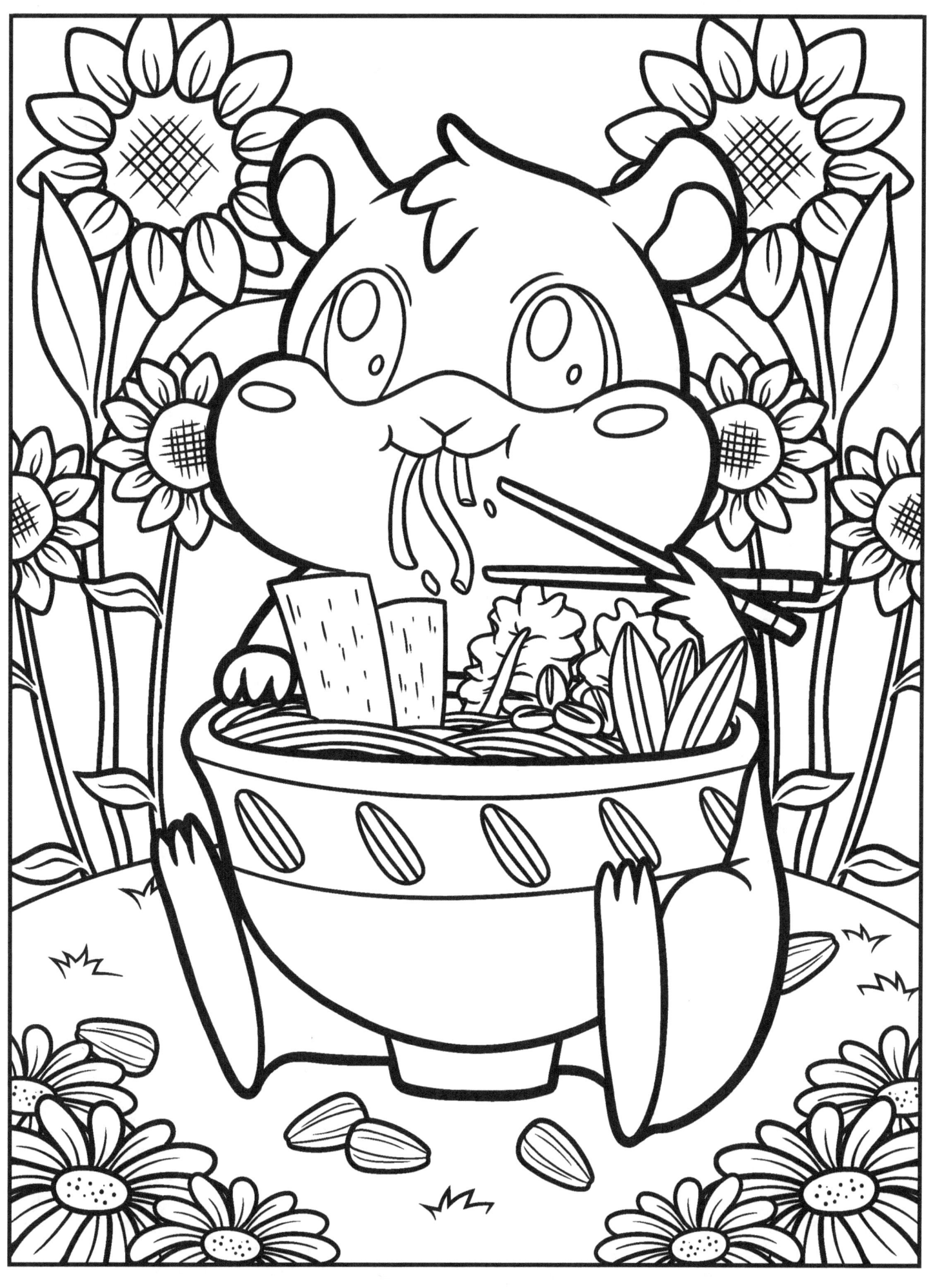

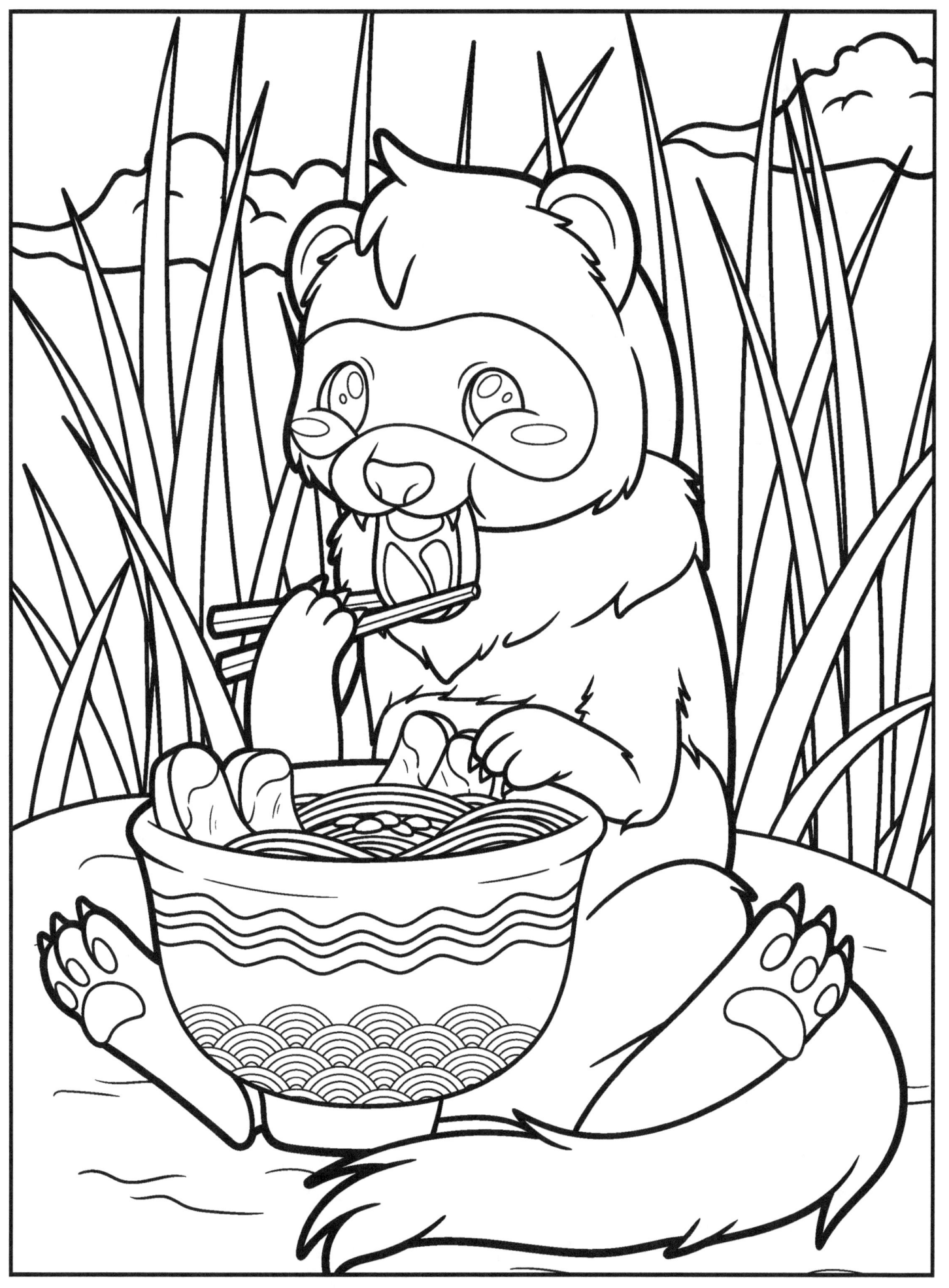

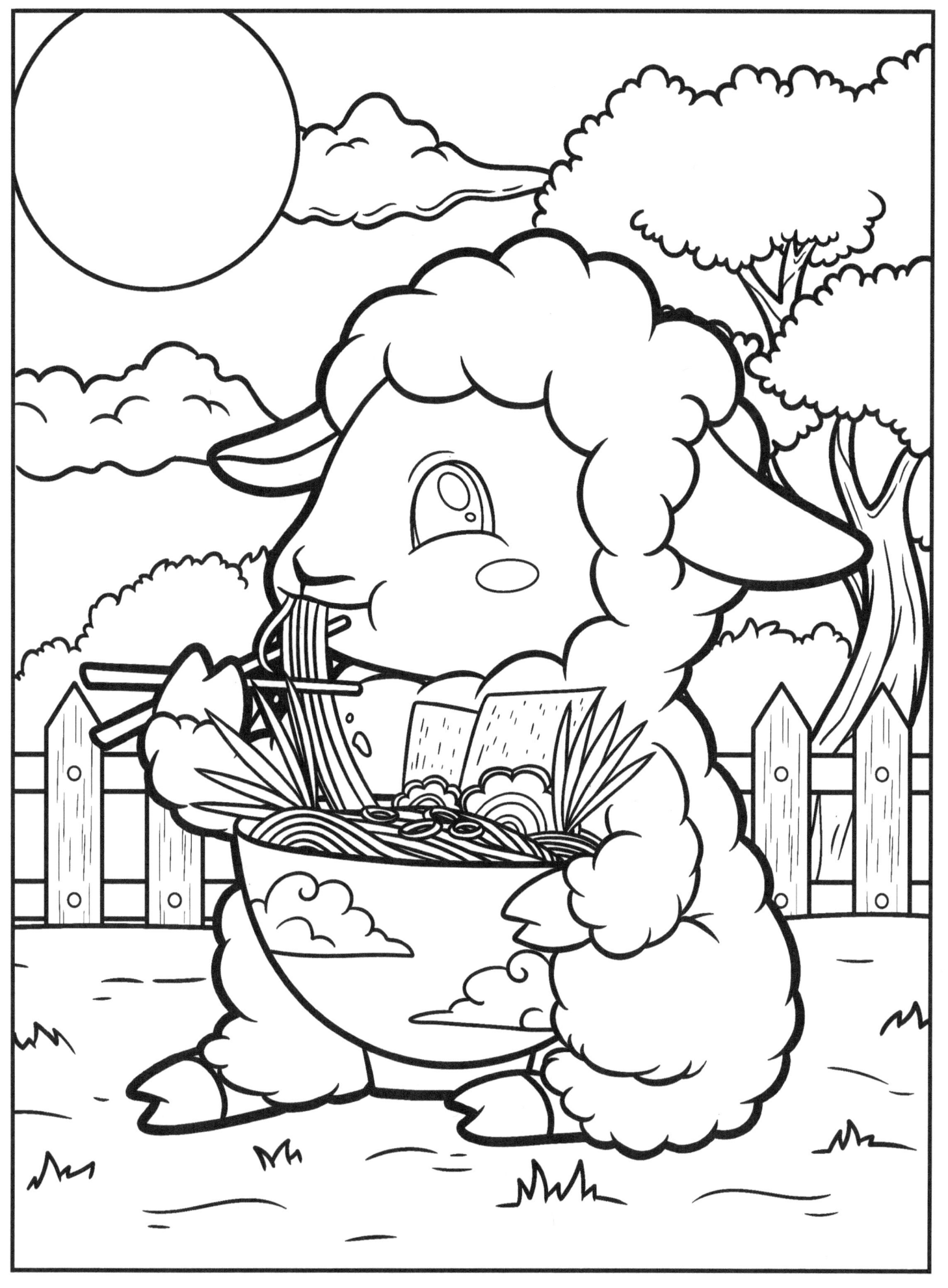

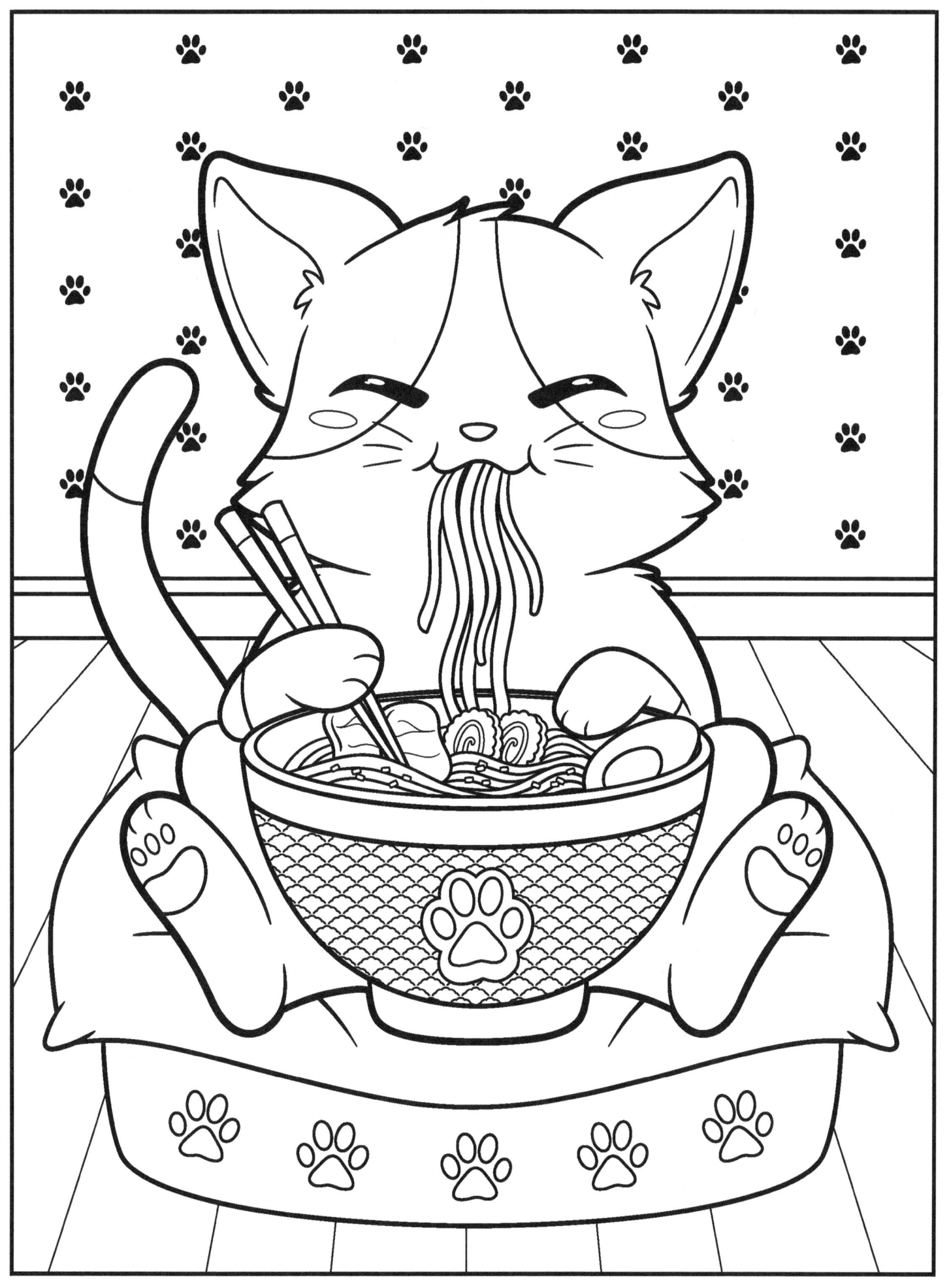

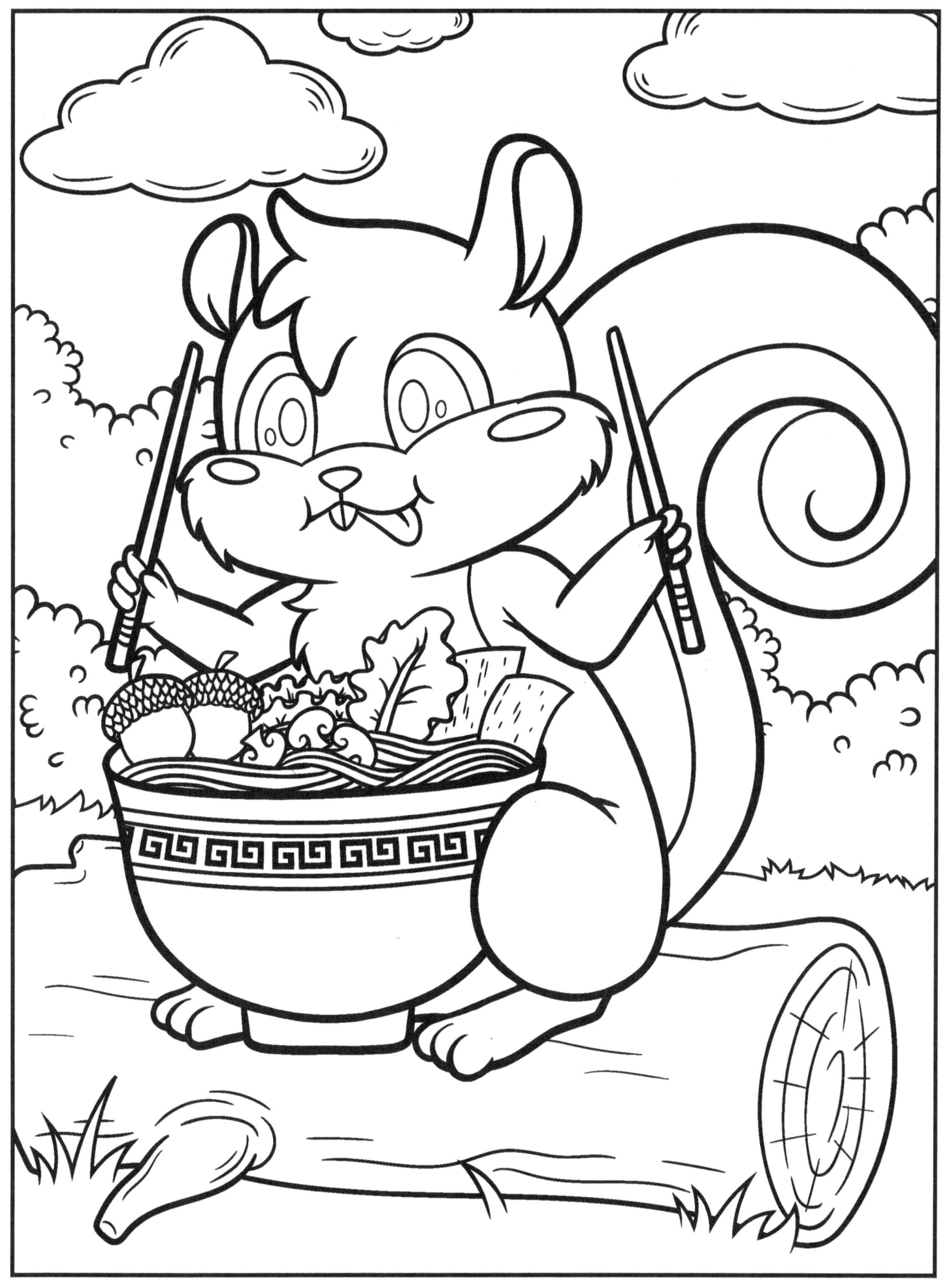

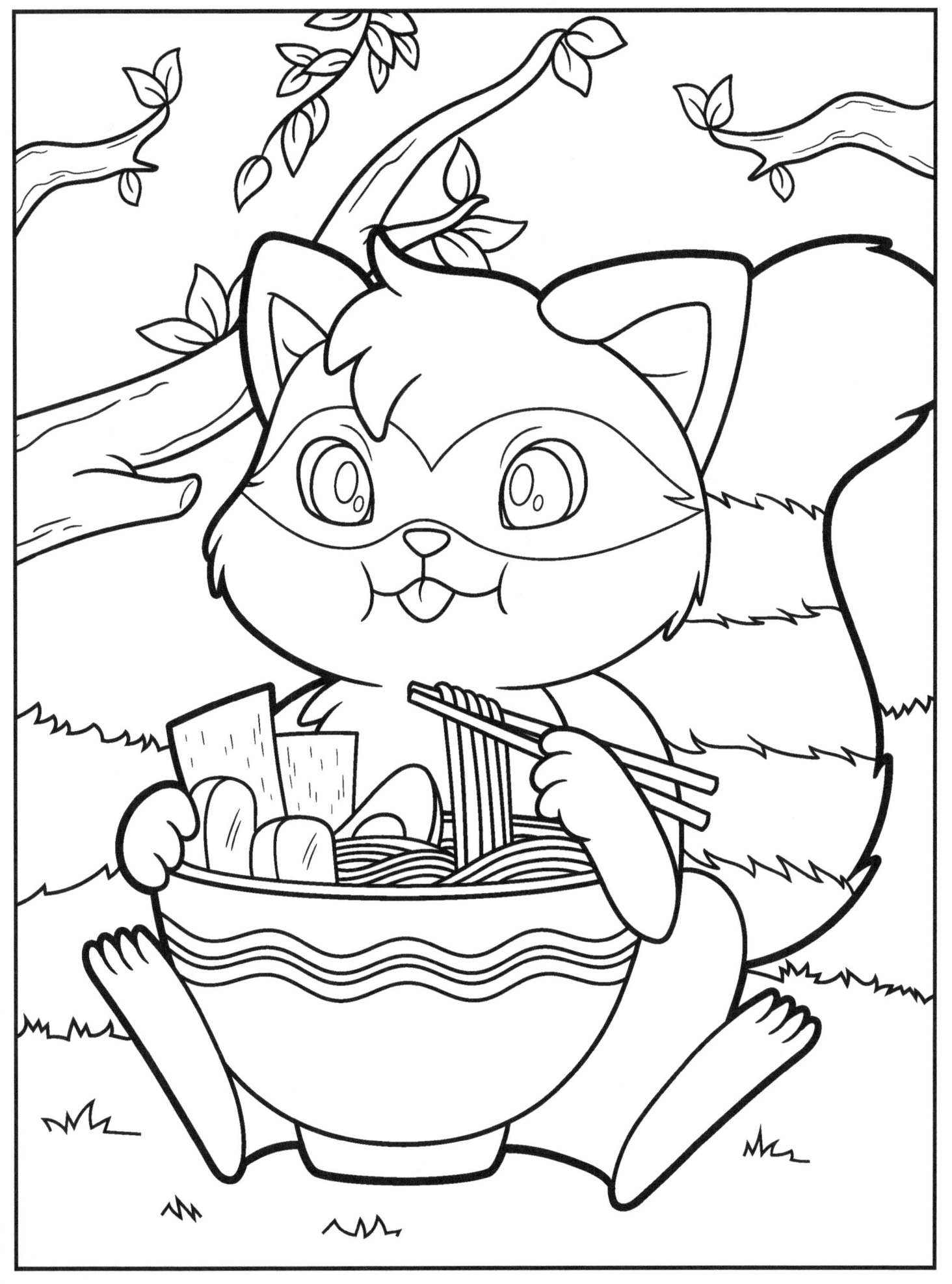

www.ingramcontent.com/pod-product-compliance
Lightning Source LLC
Chambersburg PA
CBHW081418220526
45467CB00009B/2734